Your MBA Journey Begins Here

MBA Express

By Emeritus Professor (Dr) Gary Goh

Visit website at www.garygoh.com.au

AUTHOR

Emeritus Professor (Dr) Gary Goh is a business entrepreneur and academic who work tirelessly to enrich the skills and knowledge of people, business owners and organisations.

He is revered as an inspirational educator and entrepreneur.

His skills, knowledge and experience include working as Business Owner, Executive Director, Chief Executive Officer and Consultant in diverse industries which includes accounting, auditing, aviation, construction, defence, education and training, engineering, health care, hospitality, mining, telecommunication, police, security, transport and logistics, government departments.

He has lectured postgraduate and undergraduate degree programs in universities, diploma and certificate programs in polytechnics, vocational education training institutes in Australia and Singapore.

Emeritus Professor (Dr) Gary Goh has been given awards and honours by accredited universities and government bodies around the world for his distinctive achievement in business, leadership, the learned professions, philanthropy, social justice, significant contributions to the business world, education and training internationally.

Gary's forte is the ability to identify the patterns that limit and restrict individual and business growth.

Professor Goh is dedicated to helping people to advance their personal life, career and business exponentially and grow them successfully.

ACKNOWLEDGEMENT

This book would not have been possible without the loving support of all of you who bought this book.

I would also like to thank my wife, Jasmine Koh, a truly wonderful woman.

I thank my wife for sharing the journey of developing this book with me. This book is dedicated with deepest love and affection to Jasmine. Her love and strength have allowed me to fall in love with her again and again.

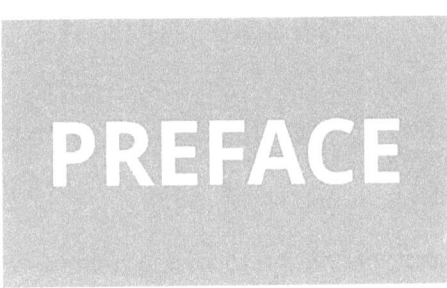

PREFACE

In today's ever-changing and highly competitive business environment, entrepreneurs, executives, managers and leaders need to be well-rounded and effectively lead their business and organizations. They must possess high-level business skills in analysis, decision making, strategy, and leadership.

The academic or case-based pedagogical approaches in MBA schools are inadequate for work experience, career, business and real life skills.

MBA Express provides practical and approachable business methodologies. This book is a fast track blend of academic knowledge and practical insights into a broader understanding of the business world and provide insights into the major areas of business performance.

Become an all-round entrepreneur, leader, manager with MBA Express.

KNOW YOUR STRENGTH

Your business or career can progress only when you exploit your strengths to the limit.
Define your goals!

To help you do that, define the following points:
• Your strengths
  These include personal, professional, experiential and education.
• Your weaknesses
  Consider all your real and perceived weaknesses.
• Your top five goals in life
  List them in order of importance.
• Your commitments
  Your commitments to family, finance and relationships.
• Your dreams
  Your ideal personal achievements if time, money, status.

Now, put all the above points into Action Plan and implement them!

ACT ON THE PLAN

Devote 80 to 90 per cent of your time using your strengths and only 10 to 20 per cent fixing your weaknesses.
Here are the steps to help you devise your Action Plan.
• Appraise your own skills
  How best do you relate to others?
• Be kind to yourself
  Don't compare yourself with others.
• Be positive
  If you can't, get out of the business or career.
• Network and grow your business or career,
  Hand out the business cards!
• Develop your faith and dream
  Faith and dream is an incredible source of energy.
• Look to your experience
  We often look at what we don't have instead of what we have.
  •Love what you do and focus on what you love.
The key in using all your strengths is to analyse, interpret and act.
We can do so much more for our business or career if we apply all our strengths.

SWOT ANALYSIS

SWOT analysis means taking a probing look at the Strengths, Weaknesses, Opportunities and Threats that face you or your business.
The analysis is a process of investigating and brainstorming the factors working for and against you or your business that could affect overall performance. Strengths and weaknesses refer to you or your business's internal advantages and potential disadvantages. These factors are in your direct control. Opportunities and threats refer to aspects outside your direct control that might open up potential (opportunities) or result in negative consequences (threats). Opportunities and threats can originate either in the market at large or from your competitors.

The purpose of SWOT analysis is to view the world in which you are performing from a macro-perspective. This vantage point ensures that the planned strategy and direction are possible, given your inherent strengths and weaknesses. It also ensures that the strategy is geared towards capitalising on opportunities and minimising threats.

S-STRENGTHS
W-WEAKNESSES
O-OPPORTUNITIES
T-THREATS

Spend a few moments now conducting a SWOT analysis for yourself or your business.

STRENGTHS

_____

_____

WEAKNESSES

_____

_____

OPPORTUNITIES

THREATS

KNOW YOUR OBJECTIVES

Setting Objectives

It is critical to write objectives for your career or business, and create a list of milestones to ensure you make progress to reach them.

What is an objective?

Objectives are concrete, tangible, measurable results or outcomes from your efforts that you can see, not just roles or activities. Well clarified objectives need to meet the following specific **SMART** criteria:

S - Specific, so that you know when you have achieved it.
M - Measurable by two or more of the following:
- Quality-specifications (Efficient? Effective? other)
- Cost.

A - Aligned with your overall vision and life or business direction.
R - Results-focused.
   Is a tangible result expected of me to produce/accomplish?
T - Time based, with a specific due date.

Too often, tasks are confused with objectives. A task is the action we take, in order to reach the objective. To differentiate between tasks and objectives, you must ask yourself:

- What are you trying to achieve by completing this task?
- What is the benefit of achieving this task?

EMOTIONAL INTELLIGENCE

Emotional intelligence conceptualises the theory that competencies based on emotional intelligence are more critical to optimum performance than intellect or technical skill.

Brilliant minds did not necessarily make brilliant individuals. It is now known that IQ on its own is not a satisfactory indication of work competence.

What also counts is EI or how well people handle everyday occurrences. There are four main interlinked:

S – Self-awareness
S – Self-management
S – Social awareness
R – Relationship management

Self-awareness:
Observing yourself and recognising a feeling as it happens;

Self-management:
Once you are aware of your own emotions, you apply that knowledge to managing your own behaviour;

Social awareness:
You are aware of how others feel, of what is seen as appropriate behaviour in your environment or role. Helps you create resonance or a positive reaction to you from other people; and

Relationship management:
Managing emotions in others, social competence and social skills.

Individuals need a balance of all four EI elements to have a significant impact on the life they led.

People are unique and need to be handled differently according to what motivates each one.

LEADERSHIP

Leaders need to:

- **Have a high IQ & EQ.** Leaders need to be able to deal with complex problems and keep track of lots of issues. They need the intellectual capacity to make good decisions in a difficult environment.

- **Be humble.** Realise that you are very lucky to have your role and that chances are you are actually not much smarter or more skilled than many other people in your company.

- **Have real empathy for others.** Realise that most staff will not be able to retire early and that they want to work hard but also have a strong family life.

- **Be good communicators:** This should be on all levels – from board members and senior managers, down to entry-level people.

- **Be open to criticism.** Solicit this from all areas and take it on board. Do not rationalise it away.

- **Be focused on the long-term benefits.** This should be for shareholders and employees.

- **Be committed.** Understand that commitment is not about working harder but about working smarter to meet goals that are sustainable over the longer term. This is a marathon; not a never ending set of sprints.

- **Having respect.** Wherever you are on the corporate ladder, you do not have permission to be rude, aggressive, or dismissive of anyone else.

- **Find fulfilment.** The happiest people are not those that have retired wealthy but those that have fulfilling jobs and the ability and resources to develop deep family and friend relationships.

- **The ability to change.** The people that can make a material change to our lives are the chief executives of the top 500 companies and government organisations. It is the CEO that sets the culture, allows people to focus on productivity and efficiency as opposed to work hours.

OFFICE POLITICS

Office politics or corporate games exist in any organization. The question is not whether you want to play or not, it is how to play it right. Some play for survival, others for power and dominance. To win is not always to defeat rivals and to lose is not always the end of the games. There are three outcomes – winning, losing and succeeding. Winning is to defeat rivals. Losing is being defeated. But to succeed is to achieve your objectives. Your aim may just be a draw on an equal and amicable win-win point. This way, all players may enjoy survival, and be successful and satisfied.

Here are some tips on playing the game right.

- **Master your position**
  Be clear of your own strengths and weaknesses as well as those of your rivals. Know your opponents well and never underestimate them. When you lay out your strengths and weaknesses side by side with others, you can plan your winning strategies accordingly.

- **Master the rules**
  Be smart on what, how, when and who to play the games against. Be aware of the risks and how far you can afford to go with them. There are no fair rules in most games. Be flexible and realistic in following the rules. Know when to listen, talk, act, compromise, negotiate and be firm. Your intuition may be the best guide.

- **Be creative and ready to adapt**
  Plan your strategy. Do you have alternative backup?
  Never play from a dead end position.
  Take a realistic assessment of the price you must pay for the rewards you will gain.

- **Don't burn bridges**
  Try your best to apply empathy and EQ to keep rivals amicable. When you keep the past clean, the future will be bright.

- **Win or lose**
  These may not be your best alternatives. The ideal one is to attain your goals amicably in a win-win draw. Give and take: compromise with rivals for negotiable terms and conditions that satisfy all. Remember, avoid ego and power struggles but focus on your job survival and success. Be a good sportsman all the time.

- **Choose the time and moves**
  Corporate games are like chess. The right timing for the right moves are vital to winning. Your patience, resilience, sensitivity, discipline and strategic planning are essential. It is not strength but when and how you apply it that counts.

- **Respond, not react**
  To react is to act impulsively and irrationally which is problem focused. To respond is solution focused with rational solution. Most errors are made impulsively but most solutions arrive from good responses. To respond well is not to fight but to flow with rivals until you gain better positions to win. Minimise your antagonism but maximise your positive personality.

- **Never outshine your boss and/or business partner**

- **Manage your boss and/or business partner**
  Establish a good working relationship with your boss and/or business partner.
  Always keep the boss and/or business partner informed.
  Do not bring problems to your boss and/or business partner, bring solutions.
  The best way to get on with the boss and/or business partner is to treat him or her as a customer. You have to exceed expectations to be a really excellent service provider.
  People who just meet boss and business partner expectations are not extraordinary.
  Reliability is being able to deliver what you promise.
  Responsiveness is the willingness to chip in when needed.
  If you are reliable and responsive, your boss and/or business partner will see you as a valuable resource.

- Never put too much trust in friends and colleagues.
- Never speak ill of your company, work, bosses, colleagues or staff

- Do not waste a lot of time scheming against others or you will be neglecting your job

- Focus your goals and priorities

- Be persistence: When faced with obstacles along the way, do not quit or look for compromising shortcuts.

Corporate games are not all bad. You can learn to be stronger, better and more fit as you strive for excellence. Remember, the fittest survives and the optimist wins. It's all in your attitude. If individuals are to live harmoniously with the environment in a natural and simple way, devoid of ambition and aggression, the world will witness a spontaneous flourishing of good fellowship and individuals would enjoy healthy, happy and long lives.

CHANGE MANAGEMENT

MAKING CHANGE WORK FOR YOU IN THE WORKPLACE

Change is everywhere around us. The amount of change in organisations has grown tremendously over the past decades. Many of these changes have been the results of new technology, societal changes, global economic changes and changes in organisational structure.

Amidst changes, here are strategies to help you work better.

- Anticipate change
  When you anticipate change and realise it will continue to take place, you can prepare for it and decide to make it work for you.

- Seek opportunity
  Without change, neither you nor I would be where we are today. Change has broaden our horizons, enabled us to grow and created new opportunities.

- Control Stress
  Some people feel stress when their companies go through organisational change or when they are entering another phase of life. Learn to control your emotions.

- Learn non-stop
  Continuous learning will help you to adapt to changes faster and more effectively. Learn not only academically but also from everyday situations.

- Build bridges
  It's common to have new people around you, a new manager or team member for instance. We tend to set up barriers to new people. Build bridges, not fences. Give new people a chance.

- Do more
  There are a lot of things to do in a change. List out the things to be done, be committed, prepare for it, set up a schedule and discipline yourself to the task.

- Be pleasant
  Nobody likes to work or live alongside a grouch, a complainer or a negative person. Be someone who has a positive attitude, who smiles, gives compliments, is considerate and shows concern for everyone else.

If you learn to accept change, tackle your goals, you will find that change is indeed a wonderful opportunity to fulfil your aspirations.

CONFLICT MANAGEMENT

MAKING CONFLICT WORK FOR YOU

Resolving conflicts is not just about solving problems. It is about soothing egos. The aim of conflict management is to create something positive out of these difficulties.

Whether at work or at home, it is inevitable that we will encounter people whose views and methods differ from our own. Some differences are minor and will not create any tension. Others of great magnitude can create constant conflict, tension and stress.

The ability to successfully resolve conflicts that stem from our differences is probably one of the most important social and organisational skills that we can possess. Unfortunately, many of us actually handle differences poorly.

Most people view differences in a negative light - as something bad that must be avoided, minimised or eliminated. Differences can also be viewed positively - as opportunities for learning and growth and for developing new social skills that can help a person to communicate more effectively with others. If managed constructively, differences can become sources of innovation and energy.

The following are four conflict management techniques that can help to calm down a heated situation and pave the way to positive action.

1. Separate the people from the problem

   When people and problems meld, emotions become entangled with the objective merits of the problem. Taking positions and refusing to let go of differences makes the situations worse because egos become identified with the positions taken. To resolve the differences, people must come to see themselves as working side by side, attacking the problem, not each other.

   Get the other party to explain his side of the story and you listen actively.
   Listen to understand the other party's point of view.

2. Focus on interests, not positions
   Your position can often obscure what it is you really want.
   Masking your true interests to maintain a certain position is not
   likely to produce an effective resolution of your differences or a
   lasting agreement for either party.

3. Invent options for mutual gain
   Free yourself from the constraints that prevent you from reaching
   optimal solutions. These may include conditions such as
   organisational pressure or the scrutiny of an adversary.
   Instead set aside a designated time frame within which you can
   discuss your differences. Create a wide range of possible
   solutions that will advance the group's shared interest while you
   reconcile the disputed issues. Make a commitment to try and
   make it work and decide what would constitute success.

4. Insist on using objective criteria

   Determine some fair standard. Avoid defensive positions and
   adamantly stating what you are willing or unwilling to do. It will
   then be possible to discuss objective criteria as well as your
   differences, so that you and the other party can achieve an
   equitable solution. Do not try to defend yourself neither party is on
   trial.

   When dealing with differences, think about the results and the
   impact your decisions will have on the other people involved. Be
   sure you are looking at the end result with a qualitative form of
   reasoning.

   Effective workers adapt their behaviour to meet the needs of their
   colleagues, subordinates and their organisation. Your
   organisation, for example, may achieve its highest productivity at
   the end of a quarter but what profit are you really making if
   workers are unhappy, resign and join your competitor. Then they
   will really be in conflict with you.

MANAGING PEOPLE

Listed are some useful guidelines in managing people.

- **Give clear instructions**
  Don't set foggy goals. Give directions in simple language. Tell the person precisely what is involved and why you think they are best for the job.

- **Listen**
  By listening and possibly helping to solve their problems, you will inevitably gain respect and get the most out of people.

- **Recognise a job well done**
  Everyone likes to know when they've done something well. Make your family members, customers and staff feel important every day.

- **Know when and where to criticise**
  Inform people when they perform well and when they don't, tell them immediately. Never criticise them in front of others.

- **Take an interest in your staff's careers**
  Coach or counsel staff on how they can climb the corporate ladder.

- **Offer a challenge**
  The best motivator is challenging work.

- **Keep communication lines open**
  Provide clear, ongoing, understandable and unambiguous communication.

- **Make staff feel important**
  All of us have the need to feel needed.

  (a) Be consistent
      Staff needs to know what to expect, so be consistent with your expectations and actions. Inconsistent behaviour breeds frustration, dismay and disappointment.

(b) Be impartial
    Do not play favourites. Discrimination destroys morale and hurts productivity.

- **Know how to say "No."**
  There comes a time when you have to say "no." Explain the reason for your refusal and avoid making a hasty decision. If possible, tell the person that you will consider the request and decide in a day or two. Take enough time to let the person know that the request has had a fair hearing. We cannot always get what we want. If you relay that to the person in a reasonable manner, you will lessen the blow.

- **Use the three magic words**

  "We," "Us" and "Our."

- **Use words that convey benefits of collaboration**

    - Brainstorm
    - Co-operate
    - Solve
    - Team
    - Together
    - Idea
    - Options
    - Cost-Effective
    - Improve
    - Effective

- **Do not use words that convey a sense of confrontation**

    - Never
    - Problem
    - Afraid
    - Cannot / Impossible
    - Fault
    - Wasted
    - Unfair
    - "I," "You," "Yours" and "Mine."

DEALING WITH DIFFICULT PEOPLE

Difficult people make your life difficult. They affect your motivation and lower
your productivity. The following are ways to "confront" difficult people.

- Identify the source of the problem. List down the actions of the person affecting you.

- Analyse how these actions affect you. Do they lower your motivation and morale, induce stress in you or cause a negative effect on your efficiency and effectiveness?

- Plan carefully your approach to solve the problem.

    - Be assertive & firm but also treat the other person with respect.
    - Do not blame the person. Point out the specific behaviour that causes the problems. Confronting someone objectively is a critical skill.
    - Arrange a suitable time and location to discuss the problem.
    - Prepare for the discussion. Spend time generating possible solutions to the problem and think of creative ways to start the discussion. Avoid a tense atmosphere.
    - Be positive
    - Thank the person once the problem is sorted out.

- Develop close and warm relationships with people.

    - Make it a point to start every work day with a warm smile. Use positive and friendly words to motivate people.
    - Help your team mates whenever you can.
    - Don't keep aloof from others. Show interest.
    - Show them how you value their friendship and how you appreciate their contributions to your team's work.
    - Be aware of other people's sensitivities. Try to see every problem from other people's point of view. Be empathetic.

- Don't be too rigid in your opinions. Listen to others. Be flexible. If necessary, change your opinions.
- Blaming others when things go wrong will produce more conflict situations. Think of ways to prevent things from going wrong the next time.

COMMUNICATION SKILLS

Communication skills are acquired more than they are inborn. You were born crying, not speaking. You learned how to speak by imitating others – that learning never end and so does getting upward communication from your employees or staff to you.

- **Practice MBWA – Managing By Walking Around**

  Find out what's happening among your people. Don't talk; just ask questions and listen.

- **Maintain an "open-door policy."**

  Let your staff or employees know that if they ever have a problem, they can come and see you.

- **Tell your employees that only bad news is the news that is not communicated upward.**

  Tell them that you want to hear the good news and the bad news.

- **Don't react badly when you hear something that is a amiss.**

  Don't "kill" the bearer of bad tidings.

- **Arrange for periodic informal gatherings.**

  Have picnics, parties, group lunches. People will tell you things at a picnic, they won't tell you in your office. Attending social gatherings makes you more accessible.

- **At staff meetings, solicit regular status reports.**

  Don't be overly judgmental of what you hear in these reports.

- **Show you're human**

  Laugh at yourselves, admit your mistakes, apologise if you've done something to hurt and employee. If they think you're human, you will be more approachable.

COMMUNICATION PRINCIPLES

1. Being clear: How to present your ideas concisely.

   The **K-I-S-S** Rule

   Keep it <u>short</u>, <u>simply</u> and <u>straight</u>

RECEIVING CRITICISM

The key to handling criticism effectively is to **G-R-O-W**.

<u>G</u>ain

<u>R</u>equest

<u>O</u>bserve

<u>W</u>eigh

1. Gain Control of Your Thoughts!

   a. Plan ahead. Prepare some positive statements (self-talk) to use when criticized.
   a. Visualize success. Daydream with a purpose!

2. Request Specifics

   a. What behaviour does he/she find offensive or undesirable?
   b. What new behaviour does he/she desire to replace it? (Use active listening skills)

3. Observe and Analyse

   a. What are the qualifications of my critic?

b. Is he/she able and willing to state specifics? If so, what are they?
c. Have I been criticized for this before? If so:

*

i. By whom - by a number of people or by this same person on several occasions?
ii. What was the context in which I was criticized in the past?
iii. How important is this criticism?

4. Weigh the Cost.

a. What will be the return on my investment?
b. How hard will it be to make the changes?
c. Will it improve the situation or possibly make it worse?
d. How much time and energy will it take?
e. What are my chances of succeeding?
f. Am I satisfied with things as they are?

GIVING CRITICISM

Before criticizing, examine your motive.

1. Why am I preparing to say these things?
2. How will my criticism help the other person and/or improve our relationship?

Responsible criticism has five characteristics. It is **C – L – E – A – R**:

Current

Limited

Expresses

Acknowledges

Re-evaluates

Current:

What is the individual presently doing wrong?

Limited:

> What specific behaviour(s) do I find offensive or
> unacceptable?
> What specific change(s) do I want to see implemented?

Expresses:

> How can I phrase this criticism so that it expresses my belief,
> opinion, feeling or perception as mine?

Acknowledges:

> How will I acknowledge this person as a unique human
> being?
> How would I feel if these things were being said to me?

Re-evaluation:

> Have I set aside a date and a specific time to evaluate
> progress toward the desired objectives?

NEGOTIATION

Here are tips that could be useful to you the next time you sit at the bargaining table.

- **CONSIDER YOUR NEGOTIATOR'S POINT OF VIEW**

  Consider and understand the other party's opinion. Do not be stuck with only your point of view. Present the benefits that will come for the both of you. By doing so, you also encourage the other party to see from your viewpoint.

- **GET 'YES' ANSWERS TO YOUR REQUESTS**

  Formulate your requests to the other party responses with a 'yes'.
  For example, say:
  "Would you like to explore other options?" or,
  "Do you think we could agree on a price that benefits both of us?"

- **DO NOT BE DETERRED BY NEGATIVE RESPONSES**

  A "no" answer need not be the end of a negotiation. Read between the lines and consider other interpretations of what your negotiator is saying. For example:
  "I cannot agree on this price" could mean "You may have to talk to my boss".
  "I cannot see how we can complete this on time" could mean "Explain how it can be done".
  "These are our usual prices" could mean "You have to give me a good reason to offer you a discount".

- **TAKE OWNERSHIP OF YOUR OPINIONS**

  Avoid offending the other party by making him feel "wrong". When this happens, people gets defensive and striking an agreement is hard. Be accountable for your opinions.
  Instead of saying: "You are too expensive" or "The quality of your product is not good".
  Substitute with statements such as "I find the prices too high in comparison with" with "I am concerned with the product quality".

- **DO NOT RUSH. CONSIDER CAREFULLY**

  Taking your time to reject or commit to a proposal is as important as your ability to think and react nimbly. Do not be pressured into reacting swiftly simply to impress the other party.

- **SILENCE DOES NOT ALWAYS MEAN "NO"**

  Do not be intimidated by pregnant pauses. The person who is uneasy with silence often rush into giving away more than he intended. This could bring a negative outcome to the negotiation.

- **DO NOT GET PERSONAL. NO ONE'S AT FAULT**

  Even if you cannot reach an agreement, do not take it personally. It is the proposal that is rejected, and the circumstances that are not ideal. It is not the persons involved that are at fault. Make notes throughout the negotiating process. Review them to learn what worked for you and what didn't. That way, you will be better prepared and more confident in your next meeting.

- **SAY "NO", IF YOU MUST**

  Opinions will differ. Avoid lengthy explanations. Give short, reasonable answers based on deadline or cost, for example. Reaffirm points of agreement before stating the differences. This helps the other party to be more receptive to your disagreements.

GOLDEN RULES OF NEGOTIATING

- Listen
- Talk about relevant issues that involve the present
- Avoid past problems
- Talk about the possible
- Avoid the impossible, or the unlikely

- Start with those issues likely to lend themselves to early solutions
- Stick to the agenda items; avoid digressions and detours
- If an impasse looks likely, table that issue and move on to the one
- Watch and be alert and sensitive to timing. If you sense the time is right for agenda item number four, skip right to it.
- Be courteous; avoid put-downs, insults, insinuations and sarcasm. Don't make fun of the other guy, be sensitive to his wants and needs
- Think and talk sensitive
- Think and talk creative solutions. Don't get locked into `doing it this way because that's the way we've always done it'

LISTENING SKILLS

Listening well is vital to communicating as talking well. When people aren't listened to, they get frustrated, invariably resulting in some form of communication breakdown. Listening to and acknowledging what other people have said may seem simple. But listening well, particularly even when you disagree with what is said, takes true talent. And as with any skill, listening well takes plenty of practice. In business today, there seems to be a growing realisation of the importance of solid listening. After all, lack of attention and respectful listening can be costly - leading to mistakes, poor service, misaligned goals, wasted time and lack of teamwork. By listening in a way that demonstrates understanding and respect, you develop rapport and that is the true foundation from which you can sell, manage or influence others.

Here are some tips on listening:

- **GIVE 100% ATTENTION**
  Prove that you care to listen by stopping all other activities.

- **LISTEN WITH EMPATHY**
  Put yourself in the other person's shoes. Everybody wants to be heard and understand, so it helps communication when you let the other person know that you are listening and not merely hearing their voice.

- **RESPOND**
  Your responses can be verbal or nonverbal like giving nods. But you must show you have received the intended message and, more importantly, that it had made the correct impact on you. Speak at the same energy level as the other person. Then they'll know they really got through and don't keep repeating.

- **SHOW YOU UNDERSTAND**
  Just saying 'I understand' isn't enough. People need some sort of proof that you really do understand. Prove it by occasionally restating the gist of their idea or by asking a question which shows you know the main idea. It's important not to repeat what they've said. Proving that you're listening and proving you understand are not the same and each

send markedly different messages when you are communicating.

- **PROVING YOUR SINCERITY**
  You can do this naturally by adjusting your tone of voice, rate of speech and choice of words to show you are trying to imagine being where they are at the moment.

- **MINIMISE DEFENSIVE COMMUNICATION**
  We listen four times faster than we speak. What often happens is that we start constructing answers or rebuttals in our minds as the speaker is talking. Try to avoid doing so and instead concentrate on listening to the message 100% of the time.

- **MAKES YOU MORE COMPETENT, INTELLIGENT, INCREASES YOUR POWER**

  The more information you have, the more successful you will be. Listening is the way to get more knowledge than most others.

- **KEEPS YOU OUT OF TROUBLE**

  Listening heeds instructions, suggestions and warnings. People rarely have cause to get upset at someone who pays attention to them.

- **TELLS YOU WHAT IS GOING ON**

  Life is a total learning experience. Things are happening around you all the time. The more you understand those things, the more you learn personally and professionally from your experience.

PUBLIC SPEAKING

THE M AND P CHECKLIST FOR PUBLIC SPEAKERS

Be mindful of:

- **MATTER** - material, facts, sources of information, insight Keep it simple, relevant and accurate.

- **MANNER** - logic, success in communicating persuasiveness, sympathy with audience. Keep it friendly and sincere.

- **METHOD** - organisation of the speech itself, ingenuity in presentation and attack. Keep it grammatical and exact.

Be persuaded by:

- **PREPARATION** - essential, no matter how experienced you become.

- **PRACTICE** - vital to every speaker.

- **PACE** - keep your delivery slow enough for your audience to follow you.

- **PAUSES** - use them well, to allow your audience to take in what you are saying, and for dramatic effect.

- **PITCH** - is necessary for your voice to carry. Project your voice so that you are heard easily.

- **PUNCH** - your delivery needs it to deliver your conviction and carry your argument. Punch comes into its own when you utter your final sentence.

ETIQUETTE

- Smile upon seeing the person. Let the smile be turned on just for the person.

- Establish and maintain eye contact. Look at that person, not down or away while either of you is speaking. However, do not stare.

- The person being addressed first should always initiate the handshake.

- Stand up for business introductions and always give a firm but not bone crushing handshake.

- Do not place your hand on top of the other person. It is a show of dominance and is considered rude.

- Deliver a sincere greeting. Consider an alternative to the traditional and often insincere, "How are you?" Try, "It's good to see you."

- Don't speak too quietly or too loudly. Speaking in hushed tones may be interpreted as a sign of insecurity. On the other hand, some people equate loudness with rudeness.

- Observe some basic rules of politeness and etiquette. Especially, don't interrupt the person.

- Always present your card with the text facing your recipient and with both hands. Do not cover the card with your thumbs, especially in Asia. The recipient by the same token should always take the time to read the card before putting it away.

- Networking is the cornerstone of our business. Every people we meet could be a potential client, candidate or business introducer. Networking involves getting out and meeting people, talking to people, being seen by people and it is a lot of work. Make a conscious effort to talk to people. Smile.

Introduce yourself to another person. Exchange name cards when appropriate. Be interested in what others have to say.

- Join organizations and associations. Join only those which you think are the most beneficial.

- Practice the art of remembering names. Be sure you have heard the name correctly. If you do not catch the name at all, ask again for it to be repeated. And if you still don't get it, ask how it is being spelled - tell him what a unique name he has, so he won't feel uncomfortable repeating his name so many times.

- Be focused. Interact enough to create a positive impression and impart some information about yourself without overselling. Knowing when to make a gracious exit is important too.

- Follow up where possible. You can follow up with a short note or phone call a day or so after the initial contact. Alternatively, you could send relevant brochures.

- Nurture your network. Pay a little more attention to those whom you can expand the relationship.

- While speaking on the phone, remember the following etiquette:

    - Communicate with one person at a time.
    - It sounds simple but when you're on the phone, it's tempting to cut corners and disregard etiquette.
    - Don't grab a ringing phone during a face-to-face meeting.
    - This sends a message that the person's presence doesn't count for much and the caller is more important.
    - Don't cut away in the middle of phone conversations to take another call or talk with someone in your office.
    - Instead, ask for permission to put someone on hold and wait for an affirmative response.

IMAGE

Your dressing shows a lot about you. It is a silence message that speaks louder than words. 55% of a person's impression of you is determined by your visual cues. The remaining 45% are constituted by the sound or tone of your voice and your choice of words. In other words, how much a person likes or dislikes you is determined primarily by your physical appeal and this is vital for your success.

The challenge now for businessman, professionals and executives is to know how to identify the image and dress level that is appropriate for the industry, job position and business agenda from day to day.

The following are the Dos and Don'ts of power dressing for men and women.

MEN

- Do have at least one classic tailored suit. The returns on your professional image will justify the investment.
- Do buy higher-quality items. They look and last better. If you're on a budget, buy fewer.
- Do have at least three white shirts in good condition.
  Shirts: Only cotton, uncrushable or invest in well-constructed shirts with crease-free fabric.
  Have colour sense: White means responsibility
  Cobalt blue gives presence.
- Do buy a selection of high-quality silk ties for different occasions. Avoid cartoon prints in ties, especially when printed on polyester.
- Do invest in an impressive sign-pen for your shirt pocket.
- Do have well-maintained leather shoes (Polish your shoes after alternate wear)
  As George Fazier, columnist for Boston Globe puts it, "Wanna know if a person is well dressed? Look down."
- Don't wear your trousers too tight or short. It plays up your weight and poor taste.
- Don't wear a shirt that is darker than your tie, except on a non client dress down day.
- Don't opt for a canvas briefcase when in a formal suit. Carry a leather one instead.

- Don't allow tell-tale nicotine stains on your teeth if you smoke.
- Try not to keep beards or moustache. They breed distrust.

WOMEN

- Do distinguish between your professional working clothes and weekend, leisure and social wear.
- Do own at least one high-quality business-like jacket, preferably with a matched skirt.
- Do make sure your business clothes fit well. Professional alteration tailors offer fitting solutions for off-the-rack clothes.
- Do complete an outfit with a few accessories for interest and to express your individuality.
- Do wear some make-up to finish your professional look.
- Do wear low to medium heeled quality leather shoes in neutral colours.
- Do carry a matching shoulder bag or briefcase.
- Don't opt for a pastel or bright coloured business suit if you want to own only one.
- Don't wear outfits with too much spandex in the fabrics. Figure hugging clothes just don't look serious.
- Don't go overboard with prints and patterned fabrics. They do little to project a cosmopolitan professional image.
- Don't have long hair hanging in your face. You lose the chance for clear communication.
- Don't forget a smart bag and pair of shoes. Soft carry-all and slinky scandals or chunky platforms can look out of place.

FINANCIAL ANALYSIS

This is a review of financial documents of an organisation to evaluate the performance of the organisation and the strength of the financial position of the organisation. These evaluations / review would enable conclusions to be made on how well an organisation is doing and its financial strengths / weaknesses.

The law requires the filing of published accounts with the relevant government authorities. The published accounts comprises of the Profit & Loss (P&L) statement, Balance Sheet and Funds Flow Statement.

Mastering accounts means understanding the three key financial statements: the profit & loss account, the balance sheet and the cash flow statement.

Profit & Loss (P& L)

The Profit and Loss Statement gives an overview of the results of the operations of the organisation. The P&L is an organisation's statement of earnings; it shows all the income less the expenses over the year.

Balance Sheet

Balance Sheet gives the financial position of an organisation at a particular point of time. It shows assets, liabilities and ownership of the organisation.
The balance sheet is effectively a listing of everything a business owns less all that it owes.

Funds Flow Statement

To demonstrate to shareholders and other interested parties how the funds within a company would change, it became the fashion for companies to supplement their annual accounts with a simple statement showing the changes. It shows the sources and application of funds, i.e. where the funds arose and where they were applied.

Cash Flow Statement

The cash flow statement is the key to understand how well cash, which is the lifeblood of a business, is being managed. The third of the key financial statements, this is the most important yet is often underused. When cash stops circulating, a business will die. The profit and loss statement shows the profits made in the accounting period, but profits are not cash – and it is crucial to know how much actual cash has been received and paid out. The balance sheet shows the often large flow of investing activities, such as the purchase of fixed assets or the acquisition of a business, but it does not reveal whether the business has an excess (or lack of) cash. The cash flow statement links the other two key statements using cash such as an objective, no-nonsense measure that is verifiable against the bank balance.

WHO ARE THE INTERESTED PARTIES?

They are:
i)   investors - wanting to know the performance and financial strength to decide whether to invest or otherwise.
ii)   creditors - to assess whether credit could be given.
iii)   shareholders – assess performance and the strength of the organisation.

ACCOUNTING RATIOS

Investment ratios show how the financial results relate to the shareholders' stake in the business.

Gross profit margin = Gross profit / Sales

Net profit margin = Net profit / Sales

Return on capital employed = Profits before tax & interest / Capital employed

Capital employed = Shareholders' fund + loan capital

Return on shareholders fund= Profits before tax & interest/Shareholders' Fund

Asset utilisation = Sales / Total Assets

Stock turnover = Sales / Stocks

Credit period = Debtors / Sales x 365

Working Capital Ratio (Current ratio) = Current Assets/Current liabilities x 100

Quick Ratio (Acid Test) = Debtors + Cash/Current liabilities x 100

Liquidity Ratio = Cash / Current liabilities

Capital Gearing = [Loan Capital/ Loan Capital + Shareholders' funds] x 100

LIFE LESSONS

On Attitude

Life is about tenacity and resilience. Every time certain doors close, you shouldn't think that's the be-all and end-all. There could be something else out there better for you.

On work
You go into college or university with a lot of passion but the moment you graduate and start to manage clients, when they put their faith in your hands, that is when it really becomes a calling.

On empathy
If you are able to bridge the silos, you become the power broker. Many times, it is about putting people at ease and that happens when they know you are their advocate and are trying to make their lives better.

On cooperation
I always tell learners this canoeing story. We need everyone aboard to row. If one person on the canoe boat decides to just watch the view, he or she is better off the boat.

ABOUT THE BOOK

In today's ever-changing and highly competitive business environment, entrepreneurs, executives, managers and leaders need to be well-rounded and effectively lead their business and organizations.
The academic or case-based pedagogical approaches in MBA schools are inadequate for work experience, career, business and real life skills.
MBA Express provides practical and approachable business methodologies.
This book is a fast track blend of academic knowledge and practical insights into a broader understanding of the business world and provide insights into the major areas of business performance.
Become an all-round entrepreneur, leader, manager with MBA Express.

ABOUT THE AUTHOR

For more information, visit his website: http://www.garygoh.com.au

Emeritus Professor (Dr) Gary Goh is a business entrepreneur and academic who work tirelessly to enrich the skills and knowledge of people, business owners and organisations. He is revered as an inspirational educator and entrepreneur.
Professor Goh's skills, knowledge and experience include working as Business Owner, Executive Director, Chief Executive Officer and Consultant in diverse industries which includes accounting, auditing, aviation, construction, defence, education and training, engineering, health care, hospitality, mining, telecommunications, police, security, transport and logistics, government departments. He has lectured postgraduate and undergraduate degree programs in universities, diploma and certificate programs in polytechnics, vocational education and training institutes in Australia and Singapore.

Professor Goh has been given awards and honours by accredited universities and government bodies around the world for his distinctive achievement in business, leadership, the learned professions, philanthropy, social justice, significant contributions to the business world, education and training internationally.

He is the author of the American published books, Health, Wealth and Happiness (Book ISBN number: 978-1-4809-9549-9), Life Lessons (Book ISBN number: 978-1-4809-7710-5), Mind Power: Unlock the Power of the Human Mind (Book ISBN number: 978-1-4809-7853-9), Live a Life (Book ISBN number: 978-1-4809-7916-1), Business Mantra (Book ISBN number: 978-1-4809-7854-6), Applied MBA Management by Application (Book ISBN number: 978-0-8059-8413-2), Fit for Life (Book IBSN number: 978-1-6513-2675-6), Success for Life (Book ISBN number: 978-1-6517-5503-7).